"'He put in the time, won my heart, and earned the right to speak.' *Highway 11* is a gentle reminder that the most important part of being a father is being present. If you want your kids to come around when you are old, read this book."
—THOMAS CLARK,
facility director, Good Shepherd Community Church

"There are so many books out there that attempt to offer parenting advice. This is different—there's no advice on offer, instead the reader is gifted gold nuggets of wisdom wrapped up in a big bow. As a mum of two boys, I lapped it up!"
—KATE NEWMAN,
lead pastor, Edinburgh Vineyard

"I've known B. J. Condrey for over a decade, initially calling him pastor while he called me friend, but through shared life experiences, he became more like a brother. His book, *Highway 11*, is a legacy filled with stories of his dad instilling godliness, confidence, and character in him. Reading it inspired me to document my own experiences with my dad and strive to be an emotionally available parent. This impactful book is worth revisiting yearly."
—CHRIS CALLAHAN,
director of relationship management, Kingdom ROI

"Life is filled with more cul-de-sacs than thoroughfares. B. J. Condrey's *Highway 11* is an excellent aid to the reader as it uses practical teachings and applications to guide us on the journey of life. I found this book to be enlightening and comforting as it addressed many concerns I had as a youth. This book touches many facets of life and is much needed as we navigate this changing world."
—EDDIE A. ROBINSON,
adjunct instructor, Hampton University School of Religion

"B. J. Condrey's own words mixed with stories of his father cut deep into my heart. It's a beautiful account of a father and son's relationship that I think all of us long for. I hope this book will challenge you the way it has me—to become this kind of father and man."
—BRANDON DUKES,
father of six

Highway 11

Highway 11

The Impact of a Father's Timely Words

B. J. CONDREY

Foreword by Bill Glotzbach

RESOURCE *Publications* · Eugene, Oregon

HIGHWAY 11
The Impact of a Father's Timely Words

Copyright © 2024 B. J. Condrey. All rights reserved. Except for brief quotations in critical publications or reviews, no part of this book may be reproduced in any manner without prior written permission from the publisher. Write: Permissions, Wipf and Stock Publishers, 199 W. 8th Ave., Suite 3, Eugene, OR 97401.

Resource Publications
An Imprint of Wipf and Stock Publishers
199 W. 8th Ave., Suite 3
Eugene, OR 97401

www.wipfandstock.com

PAPERBACK ISBN: 979-8-3852-2540-8
HARDCOVER ISBN: 979-8-3852-2541-5
EBOOK ISBN: 979-8-3852-2542-2

VERSION NUMBER 080824

All Scripture quotations, unless otherwise indicated, are taken from the Holy Bible, New International Version®, NIV®. Copyright ©1973, 1978, 1984, 2011 by Biblica, Inc.™ Used by permission of Zondervan. All rights reserved worldwide. www.zondervan.comThe "NIV" and "New International Version" are trademarks registered in the United States Patent and Trademark Office by Biblica, Inc.™

To Mom,
the pain now is part of the joy later

Contents

Acknowledgments | ix
Foreword by Bill Glotzbach | xi
Preface | xiii

1 The Birds and the Bees | 1
2 How Would You Feel? | 6
3 The *Weight* of Words | 9
4 Bar Mitzvahs and Bullet Ants | 13
5 Marriage and Race | 16
6 How Did We Hurt You? | 20
7 Wait 24 Hours | 26
8 You Can't Break What is Broken | 29
9 Setting Me Free | 32
10 The Book We Started | 35
11 A Final Word | 39

Bibliography | 41

Acknowledgments

I AM DEEPLY GRATEFUL to you, Mom, for your enthusiasm, encouragement, and guidance. From the first time I mentioned writing a book about Dad after his tragic death, you offered only encouragement. Time and time again, you read drafts of chapters, corrected me when my memory went awry, and offered seasoned wisdom on what would be appropriate and inappropriate to share. I am thankful, and my hope and prayer is that you—more than anyone else—love this book.

To my brother Clay and sister Cassie, I am also thankful. I shared the idea of this book with you once I was months into the project. From the moment I shared, you offered only support and encouragement. This was a tremendous help, and I only hope that these stories remind you both of your own sweet stories with Dad.

I can't write any book without acknowledging you, Allison. Your endless support, encouragement, extensive feedback, and willingness to give me time are invaluable. May I be the Dad to our kids that my Dad was to me. I love you.

I also owe a special thanks to Dr. Bill Glotzbach. Bill, you have stepped in and become like a father to me over the past two years. While our relationship goes back to Kansas City over 20 years ago, I deeply appreciate you as a person, a spiritual father, and a friend. Thank you for taking time out of your extremely busy schedule to write the foreword. I am truly grateful.

I want to thank Thomas Lambert and Colten Lindberg. Years ago, I shared a few of these stories one morning at the Enlightium

Acknowledgments

Academy office in Spokane. Along with one or two others, you both encouraged me to put these stories in writing and publish a book. The idea was planted in my mind that morning.

Lastly, I want to thank Brandon Dukes, Tommy Clark, Kate Newman, Chris Callahan, and Dr. Eddie Robinson for reading the book and providing endorsements as well as encouragement.

Foreword

B.J. CONDREY HAS WRITTEN a book that is heartwarming and inspiring about having the important and needed conversations between a father and son.

I have known B.J. Condrey for over 20 years. I have seen him develop from a young adult searching for the meaning of life in his Christian faith to joyfully marrying and starting his own family. What a delight it is to read a book that reflects the heart and values of a man that I respect and admire. His stories of significant encounters with his father ring true of the man that I know.

B.J. Condrey is a trusted scholar, author, and father. I anticipated reading his book because I knew that I would learn more about someone I care about, and that I would gain wisdom about the impact of timely conversations between a father and son.

This book is a not a casual endeavor but an intentional effort to capture the key parenting growth moments in Condrey's formative years. Through these reflections he offers his personal experiences as a guide to fathers. He lets us see how the ordinary encounters between a father and son become developmentally important for a child establishing a secure sense of self, and an identity of being loved.

Condrey illustrates the importance of the teachable moments that happen along the path of life. This is not a textbook meant to train a father in the science of fatherhood, but more of a heart journal reflecting the positive impact of a father who engages well with his son. One thing that stands out to me is how an imperfect father can be used in such a profound way. Condrey does not present his father as unflawed. Rather, he shows him as a good man who looks for the right times for key conversations. However, when his father misses those moments or messes them up, he is humble enough to admit his mistake and make it right.

I think many fathers are afraid that they will fail at being a good parent. This book conveys the principle that being a good enough father is what counts in a child's life; that being a father who tries and is mindful of the important moments in life is what makes the difference. The way Condrey organizes the book provides a parenting framework of key conversations that a father can anticipate and look for along the way in childhood. I found the stories instrumental in understanding and retaining these ideas. The stories reflect simple encounters that are written in a vivid way that helps me imagine the experience. I can now recall those moments in my mind's eye and connect with the parenting principle that his father was following.

I am grateful for this book. It captures the heart of a father that comes through with clarity and purpose. I recommend reading this book as a guide into the kind of conversations that will positively impact your child and mark the moments in which you made a difference as a father. I am personally inspired by the heartfelt moments between a father and son shared by the author.

Preface

Billy Max Condrey Sr. was born on September 8th, 1956. He died tragically on June 1st, 2019, while trying to cut down a tree in a bucket lift. Days before the accident, a man had come by the house and quoted him $300 to complete the job. In other words, we could still have Dad for $300. But if you knew him, he would not have paid even $3. Dad wanted to cut down that tree. It was about facing a challenge head-on, a quality that defined so much of who he was.

While I am like my Dad in some ways, I am not like him in others. For example, I would have paid $300—probably much more—to have someone come and cut down the tree. I would rather watch an expert do what they do for $300 and enjoy a nice cup of coffee with a good philosophy book in hand. My brother, on the other hand, is wired like my Dad in this respect. Why pay another person to do what you can do? A tree is not a challenge for me, but for my Dad, it was Goliath. He had to do it. He had to try. He had to conquer. But he didn't. It was his last battle.

That said, the focus of this book is not on my father's passing. While his absence is a catalyst for my writing, the heart of this book lies in the remarkable way he engaged in strategic conversations with me during my upbringing. My father consistently initiated meaningful discussions at just the right moments, each playing a formative role in shaping who I have become. As Solomon writes, "How good is a timely word" (Prov. 15:23). I want to share these stories, each time pointing out the powerful, significant, timely,

Preface

and formative nature of these talks. Before I do, I want to share a bit about Dad.

Dad was an extremely hard worker, an eternal optimist, and a dreamer. During his engagement with Mom, he told her that he would be a millionaire by the time he was 30. On their honeymoon in Acapulco, Mexico, he told her he would bring her back on their fifth wedding anniversary. Five years passed and after experiencing a heavy dose of real life and financial struggles, they celebrated number five at a local restaurant. On the way to the restaurant, Dad suddenly said: "I am sorry. I was supposed to take you back to Acapulco this year for our anniversary and I really thought that I would be a millionaire." While making these promises, he failed to inform Mom that he had felt a call to preach at a youth camp when he was 16. Eleven years later, Dad went to lunch during a revival where the preacher spoke about the Holy Spirit. He immediately returned home and said: "God has called me to preach," and explained to Mom for the first time that God had called him at the age of 16 but he had said no.

Eventually, Dad became a pastor and he and Mom started Grace Fellowship Ministries in Winnsboro, Texas, along with another couple, Larry and Judy Green. The new church plant began in our home. The Lord blessed the work and the building where the church meets now sits on East Coke Road. While the church is not the focus of the book, I do want to say in honor of my Dad that he was the same man behind closed doors that he was on stage. In short, he was a man of integrity. Stanley Grenz and Jay Smith write in their definition of integrity:

> As an ethical term, uprightness in character, authenticity; the situation in which outward conduct arises out of and coheres with sound, inwardly held moral principles. To act in accordance with such principles is to act with integrity.[1]

If integrity involves being a person of character and doing the right thing whether in private or public, then Dad was a man of

---

1. Grenz and Smith, *Pocket Dictionary*, 61.

integrity. Of course, this is only part of the story. He was not a man of integrity for the sake of being a moral person or an upstanding citizen. He was those things, but the ultimate love and passion of his heart was the Lord, and his integrity was the fruit of his love for the Lord and passionate commitment to honor God in all that he did. He was truly a man of faith. If I may use the words of Hebrews: "and by faith [Dad] still speaks, even though he is dead" (Heb. 11:4).

John Thompson, the prominent NCAA men's basketball coach at Georgetown University from 1972 to 1999, once said: "I had the greatest luxury in life—the love of a mother and father."[2] I am convinced that one of the main reasons Mom and Dad were able to love us so well was their deep love for each other. They were best friends, and it was evident that they enjoyed talking and living life together. Dad would sometimes start his day at 4 a.m. and then come home around 9 a.m. to sit and have coffee with her. The day before he died, they sat at a table in the kitchen nook (lovely windows overlooking a shaded backyard with an old oak tree and nice, green grass) and talked about who might be the best person to take over the church when he was ready to retire one day. Little did he know how relevant that conversation would be within 24 hours. It really would be only *one* day.

Dad being a great husband and wonderful father is remarkable when you consider that he did not have a good example for a father. This is an understatement. He rewrote our family's history, triumphing over a stronghold of alcoholism that extended back to his father and paternal grandfather, to become a follower of Christ, a dependable man, a loving husband, and an incredible father. Dad's life was God's grace on full display.

Dad took time to communicate with me about important topics and did not leave me to figure them out through conversations with friends, bad decisions and their consequences, media, or whatever else. Some of the moments that arose were spontaneous while others were planned. I want to share these stories. Dallas Willard writes: "The obviously well kept secret of the 'ordinary' is

2. Limbert, *Dad's Playbook*, 22.

Preface

that it is made to be a receptable of the divine, a place where the life of God flows."[3] You could say that this book is a collection of *ordinary* moments transformed by a loving, engaged father that chose not to remain silent. With his words, he created *places for the life of God to flow.* I am different because of it. He loved me well and this book is my attempt to sing his praises and help others, like myself, who desire to parent with wisdom and words.

These conversations underscore the importance of quality time, empathy, and meaningful discussions with our children. Solomon writes: "The tongue has the power of life and death" (Prov. 18:21). Thankfully, Dad used his words strategically to build and strengthen my heart, and he backed up those words by setting a good example. While this is a book of stories about how Dad used his words, the importance of him modeling those words cannot be overstated:

> Boys watch their dad intently, noting every minor detail of behavior and values. It is probably true in your home, too. Your sons will imitate much of what you do. If you blow up regularly and insult your wife, your boys will treat their mother and other females disrespectfully. . . . If you are selfish or mean or angry, you'll see those characteristics displayed in the next generation.
>
> Fortunately, the converse is also true. If you are honest, trustworthy, caring, loving, self-disciplined, and God-fearing, your boys will be influenced by those traits as they age. If you are deeply committed to Jesus Christ and live by biblical principles, your children will probably follow in your footsteps.[4]

Dad was not perfect—none of us are—but he was careful with his words, made a point to talk *with* me and not just *at* me, and set a wonderful example.

My primary aim in this book is to help men become better fathers. My Dad's example teaches us a valuable lesson: *engage in meaningful conversations with your children at crucial times.*

---

3. Willard, *The Divine Conspiracy*, 21.
4. Dobson, *Bringing Up Boys*, 69.

Preface

This requires a loving foundation that can only be built slowly and steadily over the years. My father exemplified this by being an active part of my daily life—from fishing trips and coaching my teams to regular family dinners and being there for significant events. He invested the time, won my heart, and earned the right to speak into my life.

As I matured, the relationship between my father and me evolved into a deep friendship. It is a remarkable transition when a son's respect for his father intersects with a father's recognition that parenting an adult son differs vastly from guiding a young child or teenager. In this aspect, Dad was exceptional. He adapted as I grew. He changed as I changed, expertly navigating our evolving relationship. It resulted in a deep friendship between us as two grown men, one that I still cherish today. It is also what I miss so badly.

I believe that this book can also help mothers. The impact of a well-timed conversation is something both fathers and mothers can provide. Parenting can undoubtedly be challenging and any morsel of help and hope can be a real lifeline. I believe these stories about my Dad offer just that kind of support and inspiration for anyone navigating the complexities of raising children.

Before concluding the Preface, I want to acknowledge that I have both a younger brother and younger sister. It is crucial to note that this book reflects my own perspective and experiences. While Dad had important and strategic talks with my brother and Mom had the same with my sister, it is not my place to tell their story or speak on their behalf. Undoubtedly, they have their unique tales to tell. Therefore, this book concentrates on the conversations between Dad and me.

May our good and kind Lord use these stories to encourage, inspire, and help you in one of life's greatest and most important tasks: *parenting*.

Soli Deo gloria.

1

The Birds and the Bees

IN MY SIXTH-GRADE YEAR, my family moved to another small town in Northeast Texas. Dad accepted the position of senior pastor at a small Baptist church in the country. It was his first opportunity to serve the Lord full-time in vocational ministry. It was a small church in a small community. Over time, the church began to grow, no doubt due, in part, to Dad's passion for the Lord and his commitment to growing the church. Dad loved Jesus and he loved Jesus's bride.

If you were facing the stage in the church sanctuary, there was a wooden board where attendance and offering numbers were posted each week. I enjoyed looking at it. Something objective and measurable is nice. It showed how many people attended Sunday School that morning, last week, and a year ago. Before long, it became clear that the church was growing. This is great, right? Wrong! As the church grew, the head deacon—the one who really ran the church—had seen enough. Rather than 60 or 70, the board required three digits for the current attendance. We had broken 100! Soon after, the head deacon told Dad to go fishing and not to bring any more people from the nearby town to the church.

If you know my Dad, that was a request that he simply could not grant—*Dad lived to point people to Christ.* To make matters worse, there was a business meeting one Sunday night when the head deacon verbally attacked Dad. While many things were said, one thing stood out. He told Dad that he needed to end the service on Sunday mornings promptly at noon because the Holy Spirit is a like a faucet—*He shuts off at noon.* Who knew that someone could be such an expert on the Person and work of the Spirit![1] In that same meeting, he also told Dad that you cannot push a chain, only pull it, implying that Dad was pushing too hard for them to grow.

Dad had reached his limit. He stood behind the pulpit that night and asked my Mom to take us kids and leave. Mom began to weep. I only remember seeing my Mom weep twice in my life before my Dad died. Even now, I can vividly recall where we were seated in the sanctuary and the exact path we took to the van. I kept asking Mom: "Mom, what is wrong? What is wrong?" We got into the van and drove off. It was the last time that I ever saw that building or those people again. Dad stepped down from being the church's pastor that night.

A while before this had happened, we had bought a home in a nearby town—one not too far from the church—where I attended public school. No longer living in the country, there were houses all around and a business directly behind our house. Between the business and our home was a backyard with a chain link fence and an alleyway about three feet wide between the fence and the building. One day I went into the alley to retrieve something (probably a ball) and saw a magazine. Out of curiosity, I picked it up and opened it. Inside, I found a picture that I still have not completely forgotten to this day.

Standing there frozen, I was shocked. While the battle was real, I knew deep in my heart that this was not good for me to see. After looking for a few seconds, I dropped the magazine and did not return. Winning that particular battle in Middle School may have been my most significant victory, as it is hard to measure how that single choice—and triumph—shielded me from countless hardships and devastation in both life and my future marriage.

---

1. This is written with sarcasm. Tone is often difficult to detect in written communication, so I wanted to make this clear.

Reflecting on it now, I am convinced that my Dad's talk with me about sex years before played a crucial role. The story of that pivotal conversation, which I am about to share, is perhaps my favorite to recount because of its profound influence on my life.

The sex talk occurred in fourth grade. Dad and I were driving west on Highway 11 toward Sulphur Springs in a two-tone red F-150. We were headed to a piece of land out in the country that was owned by my maternal grandparents. This was a place where Dad often took my brother and me to practice shooting targets. We had a .22 rifle with a hand-carved stock, a bolt-action .410 shotgun, and a 12-gauge shotgun.

On this particular day, my brother was not with us. As we turned off the main road and approached a gate and cattle guard, he asked if I had ever wondered about the meaning of several words, with *sex* being one of them. Despite him mentioning four or five different words in total, I cannot remember the others to this day.

I immediately responded, "The middle word."

Dad answered, "It is not a bad word."

"Oh," I replied.

After turning off Highway 11, we unlocked the gate, drove over the cattle guard, and stopped. Dad continued: "Have you ever wondered why boys and girls have different private parts?"

Refusing to throw Dad even a bone, I replied: "No."

I am sure that Dad was thinking, "Oh boy, this is not a great start." He then described the mechanics of sex in very simple terms and shared enough information to explain that this is how babies are conceived. Honestly, I don't remember this part of the conversation in perfect detail. How could I? I was receiving the most insane, mind-blowing piece of information that I had ever received up to that point in my life.

As a side note, this talk clarified something that had always troubled me. Even as a small child, the stork delivering babies on the front porch did not make sense. I would hear adults say something like, "We want two or three children." But I would think, "Why does that matter? They can't choose anyway since the stork decides." Oh, the power of cartoons! My philosopher's mind was already kicking in and questions like this bothered me. Something was awry from a logical perspective and I knew it. The sex talk helped me reject the stork theory. The universe was making more sense.

When he had finished explaining sex in a simple, age-appropriate manner, he asked if I had any questions. I could only think of one: "Does it hurt?"

This is when Dad broke from the script. He chuckled, maybe even grinned, and said: "Oh no, son, it feels good." But he did not stop there. As an evangelical Christian who believed in the authority and inspiration of Scripture and its sufficiency for all things in faith and life, Dad explained that sex is a gift only to be enjoyed between a man and a wife within the sacred context of marriage. No exceptions.

To a degree, Dad echoed the sentiments of Holocaust survivor and psychiatrist, Viktor Frankl—an author that I do not think he ever read—who believed that love is the highest goal to which one can aspire, and that genuine love is the only proper and dignified context for sexual intimacy. Frankl writes:

> Normally, sex is a mode of expression for love. Sex is justified, even sanctified, as soon as, but only as long as, it is a vehicle of love. Thus love is not understood as a mere side effect of sex; rather, sex is a way of expressing the experience of that ultimate togetherness which is called love.[2]

Granted, Frankl's view allows for sex outside of the context of marriage which goes against what Dad shared. However, Frankl makes the beautiful and important point that love is the only proper context for sex, a point that can easily be integrated within a biblical framework. Combining the biblical teaching with Frankl's words, we can say that a *loving* marriage is the only proper context for sex according to God's Word. This message took root in my

---

2. Frankl, *Man's Search for Meaning*, 116.

fourth-grade mind and heart and proved to be a powerful guide and force in the years to come.

I am deeply grateful that my Dad did not leave it to others to teach me about sex. By initiating the sex talk, Dad had the privilege of shaping my view of sex more than anyone else.

Sex is God's idea.

Sex is good.

Sex is a gift.

Sex is to be enjoyed.

But sex has its proper place.

Dad engraved these biblical truths on my heart that day. Truth be told, few things are destroying people's lives today more than sex in all of its perverted forms. My talk with Dad in fourth grade shaped my heart, wove truth into its foundation, and prepared me to know that whatever that magazine contained was not true, good, and beautiful. Dad took the time to talk to me and that made all the difference.

2

How Would You Feel?

ONE OF CHARLOTTE MASON'S foundational truths upon which her philosophy of education rests is: "Children are born persons."[1] While this may sound simple, all you have to do is pay attention to everyday conversations within earshot to learn that most of us might not actually believe this. In this chapter, I want to share a story about how Dad valued me as a *complete* person—someone with my own thoughts and feelings— long before adulthood. Before I do, a little context is needed.

Dad sensed a call to preach at the age of 16. He declined—*No thanks, Lord.* Years later, God would revisit him when my sister was born. When Mom gave birth to Cassie, my younger sister, her lungs were severely underdeveloped. At the age of 28, Dad looked through the glass of the hospital room where she was kept and prayed: "Lord, if you will save her, I will do anything you ask." Interestingly, no one knew about this prayer for over a year.

Due to the poor condition of Cassie's lungs, she was transferred to another hospital. After more X-rays, the doctor looked at them in comparison with the X-rays from the day before and said: "There is no way that these X-rays are of the same set of lungs from a day ago." But he was wrong (oh, the difference a day can make).

---

1. Mason, *A Philosophy of Education*, XXIX.

I bet you can guess what happened next. The Lord took Dad up on his promise and he surrendered to the ministry. Sometime after Cassie turned one, Dad went to a luncheon and told Mom upon his return that he was called to preach. It was then that Dad shared with Mom what he had prayed while looking through the glass of the hospital room. God had shown himself relentless, refusing to take "no" for an answer. In the words of Francis Thompson's "The Hound of Heaven":

> I fled Him, down the nights and down the days;
> I fled Him, down the arches of the years;
> I fled Him, down the labyrinthine ways
> Of my own mind; and in the midst of tears
> I hid from Him . . .
> Still with unhurrying chase,
> And unperturbed pace,
> Deliberate speed, majestic instancy,
> Came on the following Feet . . .[2]

Dad made a deal with God who was willing to "take off his outer clothing" (John 13:4) and condescend to the point of negotiating with a mere mortal—*your daughter's life in exchange for your surrender.*

Within a few years, Dad accepted his first senior pastor position at a little country church in Chapel Hill, Texas. We had to drive about 45 minutes to get there for Sunday and Wednesday services. Because this church was small, Dad was a bivocational pastor, meaning he had to keep working his full-time job while pastoring on the side. After 1–2 years, another church in Northeast Texas offered my Dad a position where he would be able to serve the Lord as a senior pastor full-time.

As Dad and I were driving home from the church at Chapel Hill one evening (it must have been just the two of us that night), he asked how I felt about the idea of moving. He gave a few details and explained that the job would require us to move away from Winnsboro, the only place I had known. I had close friends, was involved in the sports leagues in town, was close to extended

---

2. Thompson, "The Hound of Heaven."

family, and enjoyed my life there. Though the decision ultimately lay with my parents, Dad took a moment to ask for my thoughts, despite my young age. I also remember Dad asking the question in a neutral way. In other words, he did not pressure me to respond one way or another. He genuinely wanted to know what I thought and how I felt about the possible move. After all, he could have mentioned that this was his dream, that he really wanted to do this, or even that it was what the Lord wanted—*but he didn't.* I had a desire to please my parents, so if he had nudged me in any direction, it would have made it very difficult for me to be honest with my thoughts and feelings. Thus, I admire that he did not attempt to sway my response, but only listen. Although I was young, he treated me as a full person.

I clearly remember telling Dad that moving was alright with me, feeling neither sadness nor surprise. In the sixth grade, my world orbited around my parents and siblings; they were my everything. While I loved and appreciated friends and extended family, *home* was wherever we five were together.

While this may not seem significant to some, the fact that I remember it over 30 years later when I have forgotten so many other things says otherwise. While my parents could have decided without consulting me, Dad took the time to stop, ask a thoughtful question, and wait for my answer. My thoughts and feelings genuinely mattered to him. The implicit message that came through loud and clear was: *I am an important part of this family. My voice counts. My opinion matters.*

In Charlotte Mason's words, Dad treated me as a full person, not one in the making.

3

The *Weight* of Words

MOST OF US HAVE heard, "Sticks and stones may break my bones, but words will never hurt me." Whoever coined this line was mistaken. I do not recall moments of being struck by sticks or stones, but I vividly remember certain words spoken to me—both positive and negative—from years past. While physical wounds tend to heal, emotional scars often linger. Both the words we speak and the words we don't speak matter. It is no wonder that Solomon, Jesus, Paul, and James (the brother of Jesus)—all writing and speaking at different times in redemptive history—emphasized the importance of words. You cannot read the Bible for an extended period without noticing that words play an integral part in our discipleship journey. *Words matter to the Lord.*

On average, people speak approximately 16,000 words every day. While some sources state that women speak significantly more than men, additional research has proven otherwise. In an eight-year study conducted at the University of Arizona, Matthias R. Mehl—psychology professor and the study's lead author—reported that "women spoke 16,215 words a day, while men spoke 15,669." The difference is, in statistical terms, insignificant.

What is important is the 16,000-word estimate. This is a large quantity of words. Over the course of a year, this comes to almost six million words. Over 70 years, 16,000 words a day results in 408,800,000 words. That is not far from half a billion words.

Yet, the sheer quantity of our words is not what is important, is it? Solomon counsels "let your words be few" (Ecc. 5:2) and James, the brother of Jesus, writes that we should "be quick to listen, slow to speak" (James 1:19). From a spiritual, moral, and relational perspective, quality counts much more than quantity. What we say is much more important than how much we say. It also needs to be said that what we do not say is just as important. In matters of communication, we're presented with multiple options:

1. Speak words that give life
2. Speak words that tear down
3. Silence: Refrain from speaking words of life
4. Silence: Refrain from speaking words that tear down

Depending on the circumstances, both speaking and silence—the giving and withholding of words—can deliver life or death. *Words either uplift or undermine. Words either nurture or negate.*

Solomon writes: "The tongue has the power of life and death, and those who love it will eat its fruit" (Prov. 18:21). Echoing this wisdom about a millennium later, Paul the apostle writes: "Do not let any unwholesome talk come out of your mouths, but only what is helpful for building others up according to their needs, that it may benefit those who listen" (Eph. 4:29). If words are this powerful, how much more powerful are they when coming from a parent? While some moments like the birds and the bees talk may be planned, other opportunities for a parent to step into the void and chaos appear spontaneously. This chapter is about one of those moments—an *unplanned* moment.

After Dad stepped down as pastor of the church in Northeast Texas, we found ourselves living in an old house. It was so old that we had to tear wallpaper off of the ceiling. Yes, you read that correctly—*the ceiling*. Strings then hung from each nail that had to be burned off. Luckily, I was old enough to qualify for such a glorious task which required climbing a ladder with fire in my hand and burning the strings on the ten-foot ceiling.

But I did more than burn strings! The house had a small carport where I had a weight bench. At the time, I was playing football, basketball, and baseball. We had a basketball goal out by the driveway and 10–20 Middle School boys, including me (I was 13 or 14 at the time), could be found playing out there on any given day. I think that is when I began to love basketball more than other sports.

As a result of playing football, I was required to lift weights at the school. As if this was not enough, I enjoyed having my own weight bench. One afternoon, Mom and my two siblings were gone. Dad was there and I wanted to see how much I could bench press. To max out, you need someone present to avoid the dangerous situation of being trapped under a heavy weight you are unable to lift. I do not remember how much weight I had on the bar that day. Whatever the amount, it does not matter. I remember having the clear expectation that I should be able to lift the amount on the bar and believed that anyone my age should be able to do so. For these reasons, I was devastated when I could not get the bar off of my chest.

I felt weak.

I felt pathetic.

I felt a deep sense of self-hatred for what I considered an utter failure of strength. The anger was palpable.

At that moment, Dad intervened. I still remember exactly where he was standing in the carport. After asking what was wrong and listening, he remarked: "Son, that is a lot of weight for your age."

His words immediately took root in my heart. I suddenly felt different about the amount of weight I could and couldn't lift, and more importantly, myself. The thought process in my mind was simple: "If Dad thinks I'm strong, then I am strong." This simple logic clearly demonstrates the crucial role of a father and the *weight* of his words. In the carport that day, Dad's words were more powerful than my thoughts and emotions.

That was all it took. I went from feeling deep self-hatred to being totally at peace within minutes. Dad had spoken, and what he said about me carried more weight in my heart than my self-talk. His words took precedence. They were heavier, higher, deeper, and more substantial. This experience and the weight of my Dad's words remind me of what David writes in Psalm 29. The psalm is essentially a meditation on God's voice. God's voice is "powerful" and "majestic" (v. 4). God's voice "breaks the cedars," even the cedars of Lebanon (v. 5). The list continues until we reach verse nine. What is interesting is that there are multiple translations. The NIV reads, "The voice of the Lord twists the oaks and strips the forests bare" (Ps. 29:9). Similarly, the New Living Translation reads: "... twists the mighty oaks." Other translations are significantly different, no doubt owing to what is probably a difficult passage in Hebrew to translate. The English Standard Version (ESV) and New American Standard Bible read, "The voice of the Lord makes the deer give birth. . ." It is the last translation that I love. Is the Lord's voice powerful? Yes. Can it break up the hard ground? Yes. But can it also create and release life? Yes! The voice of the Lord even causes deer to give birth. He is a life-giving God and his words are the primary vehicle by which he delivers this life.

This is one of those talks that was spontaneous. Yet, Dad was ready all the same. He did not miss his short window—one of those windows that opens suddenly with no prior warning—to speak life-giving words. He stepped into the void—my emotional chaos—and spoke words that pierced my heart. They were sharp, effective, and timely. I am convinced that the primary responsibility of a father on earth is to reflect the Father in Heaven. Therefore, it is no wonder that a father's words carry great influence and profound impact in a child's life. Those few words in the carport that day completely changed how I felt about myself. Dad was present and willing to speak, and that made all the difference.

4

Bar Mitzvahs and Bullet Ants

IN JEWISH TRADITION, THE Bar Mitzvah is a significant rite of passage for 13-year-old boys. It marks the age at which a boy is considered to have reached religious maturity and is responsible for his own actions in terms of Jewish law, tradition, and ethics. The ceremony typically involves the young man reading from the Torah (Jewish holy scripture) for the first time in front of the congregation, symbolizing his transition into adult religious responsibilities. Following the religious ceremony, it is common to have a celebratory meal or party with family and friends. It is an extremely important moment in a boy's life as he transitions into manhood with the full authority and support of the community.

Other coming-of-age ceremonies seem a bit more harsh. The Sateré-Mawé people who live deep in the Amazon have a ritual for young men. The Smithsonian Magazine reports:

> Boys as young as 12 years old must gather bullet ants from the forest, which are then used to make ant-ridden gloves. The young men wear the gloves 20 times for 10 minutes, performing a dance while those angry insects sting them. . . . the bullet ant's sting is supposed to be 30

times more painful than that of a bee, and each of those gloves contains dozens of ants.[1]

Why such a ritual? The author continues: "The ceremony, the tribe chief says, is meant to show the men that a life lived 'without suffering anything or without any kind of effort' isn't worth anything at all."

Unfortunately, nothing like this exists in American culture. Don't misunderstand me—*bullet ants are not my style*. That said, there is something special about a young person being able to look back and mark when they were initiated into adulthood. Having a coming-of-age process requires a community vision, a shared understanding, concern for the younger generation, and intentionality. Surely there is great emotional and spiritual power in being called by the elders of one's community from boyhood into manhood.

While there was no Bar Mitzvah or bullet ants, I do remember a talk with Dad that indicated something had changed and that Dad no longer viewed me as a mere boy. Unlike most talks, I do not remember where we were when it occurred. It was during the early part of my 9th-grade year in High School, so I was probably 14 or 15. Dad led by saying that there would be times when we would disagree over the next few years—conflict was inevitable. However, Dad assured me that it was nothing to fear. He went on to say: "I don't mind you disagreeing with me in the next few years. Whether you are upset with me or whatever, I can take it. The only thing I require is that you be respectful at all times when voicing your disagreement or frustration."

This sounded fair to me. I also remember feeling that something had changed. A shift had occurred. Dad granted me present and future permission to have my own ideas, be upset, feel negative emotions, disagree with him, and be honest. His only expectation was that I communicate my opinions and feelings in a respectful manner. However, this was not all. He changed his tone to make his final point that while he would give me some leeway as I found

---

1. Nuwer, "When Becoming a Man."

my way and matured, he would never tolerate disrespect in any form toward Mom. In typical Southern fashion, he liked to remind me that our Mom was his wife.

At a glance, this might suggest that Mom was weak or could not stand up for herself, but this is not what Dad meant. Matter of fact, I gave Mom the nickname "Red Bug" in my 20s. She is a redhead and can be quite fiery! She did not need my Dad to protect her from disrespect; she could easily hold her own. Nevertheless, Dad's refusal to tolerate any disrespect towards her was one of the ways he demonstrated his love toward her. In a typical complementarian fashion, he believed it was his role to be the spiritual leader of the home, and in this case, it meant drawing clear boundaries on what would and would not be allowed.

I am thankful for this conversation that served as a rite of passage. While I did not read from the Torah or get bitten by ants, I knew that something had changed. I was transitioning into manhood, and Dad both affirmed and welcomed this reality. Once again, Dad engaged, and it made all the difference.

5

Marriage and Race

WHILE THIS STORY COULD be told without much detail, I want to explain the racial climate in Winnsboro, Texas during my High School years. This will help place this story in context.

In the 1980s and 1990s, Winnsboro was a segregated town. Most black people lived in one part of town while whites lived everywhere else. At the time, Winnsboro was probably 95% white or more. At age 5 (1983–1984ish), I was preparing to play organized baseball in our town's little league for the first time. I was destined to be a T-ball star. I still remember WeWe, my maternal grandmother, paying me one dollar for every pop fly that I caught at shortstop. If you have ever watched a T-ball game, you know that pop flies are a dime a dozen. If I had been smart with my money and invested it with interest, I probably would be a millionaire by now.

The day came when the T-ball coaches gathered and drafted players. They drew names to see who would go first. They moved through the list of boys' names and at the end, only two remained. They were black. The other coaches did not want them mainly because it would mean having to pick them up and take them home for every practice and game. In short, it would require a lot of extra work. This is what they said. Dad stepped up to the plate and said: "I'll take them."

I am really grateful that Dad drafted the two boys (withholding names out of a respect for privacy) because it allowed me to interact with and build friendships with people of a different race. In a town that is predominantly white and somewhat segregated, it is easy to avoid those who are different from you. But at the age of five, Dad opened the door for me to learn that all kids possess equal and intrinsic value for the simple reason that all are created by the same loving God. On the pitch, you are just a group of kids trying to win a game and you root for each other because you are on the same team chasing the same goal. This also serves as a great reminder of why sports can play such an important role in the moral formation of children and young adults.

Fast forward several years when I was a junior in High School. I had quit every sport except basketball because of my love for the game. Of the 8–10 players, four were black and two of the four were the same boys that Dad had drafted years ago. Again, I am thankful for sports. Participating in sports made it impossible for me to do what many in small rural communities often do: avoid interacting with people of another race. One day, I drove up to the school and noticed a lot of activity. Someone had come to the school during the night and hung a black doll from the flagpole. At our High School, the flagpole was front and center; it was the first thing you saw when you walked toward the front doors. During the night, someone had tied a black doll to the rope—*a hanging*—and then pulled the rope to raise the doll to the top of the pole. For a few hours, it hung in place of the American flag. The doll was immediately lowered and replaced that morning, but the message was clear: *there are white folk in this town and school who would still hang you if possible*. In all "fairness," there are those in every town throughout the South.

I share these stories to paint a clear vision of the racism in Winnsboro, Texas in the 1990s so that there is appropriate context for both my Dad's words and their significance years ago. After finishing my undergraduate degrees at the University of

Missouri-Kansas City, I returned home to Winnsboro at the age of 25 to serve as a youth pastor under my Dad's leadership. He was the founding and Senior Pastor of Grace Fellowship Ministries. Because it was a small church and we both wore many hats, we spent a significant amount of time together. One day, we were in the truck—it is amazing how many talks happened in a truck[1]—and Dad said something that I never forgot: "B.J., I want you to know that I do not have any problem with you marrying a black woman." We were not even talking about marriage at the moment, so it came as a surprise.

He continued: "If you can look at me and say, 'Dad, I have prayed and sought the Lord and this person really is the one that God has for me,' then that is fine with me . . . . I am okay with it." Not much more was said about the topic, but the message came through loud and clear. I was free to follow God's leading rather than any false path informed by a cultural narrative dominated by racism and fear.

Without the backdrop of my early years in Winnsboro, this conversation might seem peculiar or potentially unsettling, especially to black individuals. I sincerely hope that it does not come across that way. This is why I have taken the time to describe the racial climate in Winnsboro during my childhood. Only with this understanding can one truly grasp the significance of my father's words to me—words that, in their context, were incredibly forward-thinking, courageous, and reflective of a spirit far removed from prejudice. It is only when one understands that climate that one can truly appreciate Dad's words in all of their fullness and how revolutionary, bold, and non-racist they were. It was another

---

1. When two people are in a vehicle, they are side-by-side rather than face-to-face. In writing this book, I realized how many of our talks were in a truck with Dad and me side-by-side. It reminds me of C.S. Lewis' words on friendship: "Hence we picture lovers face to face but Friends side by side; their eyes look ahead" (Lewis, *The Four Loves*, 786). Since several of my talks with Dad were on important and sometimes intimate topics, I wonder if the truck made it easier for both Dad and me to talk in detail due to us being side-by-side rather than looking directly at each other. Of course, we would look at each other at moments but could always return to our forward gaze.

talk that I remember to this day. Dad chose to use his influence to liberate me, ensuring that the Lord was my shepherd when it came to making one of the most important decisions of my life.

6

How Did We Hurt You?

OVER THE PAST FEW decades, psychologists have determined that there are four parenting styles. Citing the work of Lisa Kakinami, psychologist David Myers writes: "Parenting styles can be described as a combination of two traits: how responsive and how demanding parents are."[1] The four styles are as follows:

> *Authoritative* parenting is often considered the ideal style for its combination of warmth and flexibility while still making it clear that the parents are in charge. Children of authoritative parents know what is expected of them. Their parents explain reasons for the rules and consequences for breaking them. Parents also listen to their child's opinions, but the parent remains the ultimate decision maker.
>
> *Permissive* parents might pride themselves on being their child's best friend. These parents are warm and nurturing with open communication. They are actively involved in their children's emotional well-being. They also have low expectations and use discipline sparingly. Permissive parents let children make their own choices, but also bail them out if it doesn't go well.

---

1. Myer and DeWall, *Psychology in Everyday Life*, 88.

Authoritarian parenting uses strict rules, high standards and punishment to regulate the child's behavior. Authoritarian parents have high expectations and are not flexible on them. The children might not even know a rule is in place until they're punished for breaking it.

Neglectful parents fulfill the child's basic needs, but then pay little attention to the child. These parents tend to offer minimal nurturing and have few expectations or limitations for their child. It's not always a conscious choice parents make, but can be forced by circumstance, such as the need to work late shifts, single parenting, mental health concerns or overall family troubles.[2]

The consensus in psychology is that the authoritative style is the best. As one source states: "Authoritative parenting results in children who are confident, responsible, and able to self-regulate."[3] On the contrary, other parenting styles have been shown to affect children in all sorts of negative ways. There is one study that even shows a correlation between parenting style and childhood obesity. The study found that, compared to children with authoritative parents, those with authoritarian parents had a significantly higher chance of being obese—35% for preschool-aged children and 41% for school-aged children.[4] There are also correlations between permissive parenting and children being more aggressive and immature, neglectful parenting and children with poor academic and social outcomes, and authoritarian parenting and children with less social skills and lower self-esteem.[5]

Needless to say, this topic is no small matter. Looking back, I can see a small dose of the authoritarian parenting style when my Dad would say things like, "Because I said so." The basic idea is to not ask questions, do what you are told, and obey. That said, I think this was more the case when I was really young. For most of my childhood, teenage years, and into adulthood, I remember Mom and Dad parenting with an authoritative style. This transition is

2. Nelson, "The 4 Types of Parenting Styles."
3. Sanvictores and Mendez, "Types of Parenting Styles."
4. Kakinami et al., "Parenting Style and Obesity Risk in Children," 20.
5. Myer and DeWall, *Psychology in Everyday Life*, 14.

not uncommon. I have taught Psychology and AP Psychology at the High School level and students often reported that their parents' style of parenting changed as they grew older. I think that this makes sense to some degree. While it may be important to lay the groundwork and instill an understanding of authority and obedience when a child is really young, it is equally important to shift at some point and make way for the relationship to be more conversational even about rules and consequences.

Drawing from the above description, Mom and Dad would often give reasons for the rules and consequences for breaking them, allowing me to speak and explain myself when applicable and listen to my opinions although it remained clear that my parents were the ultimate decision maker. I believe that their Authoritative (not Authoritarian) style of parenting is one of the main reasons that I enjoyed such a great relationship with my Dad throughout my life until his death. He loved me, appreciated our differences, genuinely asked my opinion at times, and treated me as a fellow man/adult once I moved into my later teenage years and on into my 20s and 30s. This laid the foundation for a meaningful friendship that profoundly enriched my life. As C.S. Lewis writes: "Friendship is unnecessary, like philosophy, like art, like the universe itself (for God did not need to create). It has no survival value; rather it is one of those things which give value to survival."[6]

This played a significant role in the talk that I now want to share. I was home from college one summer and my parents and I were talking in the kitchen. While Mom was busy preparing something tasty, Dad and I sat at the table. Unfortunately, I don't remember how the conversation began or what we were talking about, but there was a decisive shift. Somehow the conversation turned to the fact that parents can unintentionally do things that hurt their children. After all, no one is perfect. At that moment, Dad looked at me with a light but serious tone and asked: "Did we hurt you in any way?" I remember Mom immediately responding, "We didn't, did we?" There was deep concern in her voice. She had devoted her last 20 years to being a homemaker and giving us

---

6. Lewis, *The Four Loves*, 789.

children the best life possible. In my view, I think the question felt more threatening to her, and understandably so.

Truth be told, I had wanted to talk to my Dad for years about something from my childhood that was extremely difficult for me. Yet, how do you initiate such a conversation? How do you tell someone that you love, admire, and respect that they failed you in a particular way? For better or worse, I had decided years before that day in the kitchen that I would not initiate this conversation with Dad. In Psalm 16:8, David writes: "I have set the Lord always before me" (English Standard Version). The Lord would have to go before me, open the door, and hand me the opportunity.

The Lord did. I knew in the moment what God was doing. What unfolded next is still to this day one of the most beautiful moments of my life. I looked at Dad and said: "Well, there is something that I have wanted to talk to you about for a long time. There was something that you did when I was younger that hurt me." Dad reassured me that he wanted me to share. I remember feeling safe and loved. My parents had truly placed the welcome mat before me.

As a child, there were times when Dad was frustrated with me over something I had done. I have one distinct memory from when we lived at 605 Meadow Drive in Winnsboro. The room that my brother and I shared had two big closets, so Dad used one of them. I had done something wrong and was sitting on my bed waiting for Dad. He came in, walked into his closet, said a few things in response to my behavior, and then exited the closet and walked out of the room. It all happened so fast. I remember feeling his disapproval at a deep level.

While this might not seem like a big deal, it happened on more than one occasion. I would do something wrong that required discipline but Dad would not always stop to talk. Now that I am a parent, I get it. Life is busy and an adult's plate is full. When you have several kids and these moments pop up throughout the day, it is hard to address each one in a thoughtful manner. I surely don't although I am doing my best.

That said, Dad would at times express disapproval and move on (if I was not also being spanked). In those moments, I was left sitting alone with my thoughts and a dose of shame. I had let my parents down and as so many first-borns know, this was devastating to me. I wanted their approval and it brought me great joy to please my parents. Yet, when Dad walked out of the room without us pausing and having a chat, the situation felt unresolved emotionally. Looking back, I realize now that I process things verbally. This explains why it was so challenging for me at times when I could not discuss matters with Dad.

Fast forward a few years and my emotional response began to change. While I would still internalize the disapproval, I began to experience less shame and more anger in my late pre-teen and early teen years. However, my response was the same—*to keep it in*. I did not want to be disrespectful.

I do want to state for the record that Dad did not always respond this way, and honestly, I do not remember this type of response nearly as much in my mid to late teen years. For this I am grateful! But it does not change the fact that it did happen from time to time during my childhood and preteen years, and it affected me.

That day in the kitchen, I shared honestly. I shared how I felt so much shame when he walked out of the room with things unresolved. I shared how I wanted him to sit beside me, look at me, and have a conversation. I then explained how that shame morphed to anger as I got older. As a testament of his love, humility, and maturity, he sat and listened. By this time, Mom had stopped what she was doing and was sitting at the table with us.

He did not deny anything.

He did not make me feel like anything was my fault.

Instead, he listened without interrupting and then humbly asked if he could share what he was feeling in those moments when he walked away because he believed it might help my heart. In a remarkable display of vulnerability, he first apologized and then confessed that he was aware in those moments that he was walking away and that it was not best for me. In a startling admission, he voiced that he felt shame over how he responded to me. He knew that he had responded in a short, frustrated tone, and knew it wasn't best. Once he realized what he had done, he didn't know what to do next. It was easier to keep walking and not return because he was displeased with how he had handled the situation. He was aware of his failure to stop and be present in those moments and then allowed the guilt to drive him right out of the room, leaving me alone with whatever I was feeling.

On this special day in my early 20s, Dad had the love, courage, and humility to open a door and invite me to speak freely. Henri Nouwen writes:

> We are healed first of all by letting [memories] be available, by leading them out of the corner of forgetfulness and by remembering them as part of our life stories. What is forgotten is unavailable, and what is unavailable cannot be healed.[7]

You could say that he invited me to make my memories—at his own expense—*available* that day which in turn made healing possible. It was a gift. In my view, this is one of the most important stories I share because I wonder how many parents have the humility and courage not only to admit their mistakes, but also to take the next step and provide their child a safe space to share freely. Let's be honest: *We are all making mistakes as parents. We are all getting it wrong at times.* What Dad did for me that day brought healing and made a significant difference in my life.

People hurt us, and then God turns around and uses people to heal us. In this case, it was the same person.

---

7. Nouwen, *The Living Reminder*, 22.

7

Wait 24 Hours

IN MY EARLY 30S, I was living in Picayune, Mississippi with my wife, Allison. We had purchased our first home with 1.5 acres of land out in the country. I was serving as a youth pastor and did not have the money to buy a riding lawn mower. This meant using a push mower with a 20" cut to mow the grass. It was quite the chore and took more time than desired although I do enjoy cutting grass (within reason).

Picayune is about 500 miles from Winnsboro, Texas, where Dad and Mom lived. If you drive it hard without making many stops, it takes about eight hours. They were about to come visit us and Dad called and asked if I wanted to purchase my grandmother's John Deere riding lawn mower with a 42" deck after my stepgrandfather had passed. Unfortunately, I told him that we did not have the money but that I appreciated the offer. That is where the conversation ended.

Weeks later, I was standing outside when they drove up. Before they pulled off the main road, I saw a green and yellow riding lawn mower in the back of the truck. They gave it to me as a gift. It truly met a need, and I was so thankful. Few things bless the heart more than another's act of generosity.

They stayed for four or five days. As always, we had a wonderful time. It was during that visit that something else happened that created yet another opportunity for Dad to speak into my life. I received a phone call from someone informing me about one of our leaders in the youth ministry. Their behavior had fallen significantly below the moral standard that was required; I was very angry. When a leader welcomes compromise, it can have devastating effects on so many people, especially teens.

After the conversation, I told my Dad that I needed to make a phone call. In a gentle and calm voice, he asked: "Can I give you a piece of advice?" I remember his tone being respectful. He was not going to push anything at me but simply asked for the permission to speak into my heart. Similar to the ninth-grade conversation discussed in another chapter, his approach affirmed that he was approaching me as both a fellow adult and co-minister. With a bit of sarcasm, I answered: "Sure."

Dad then suggested that I follow his rule: "B, when I get really angry at someone, I force myself to wait 24 hours before initiating a conversation with them. That gives me time to cool off so that I do not say something that I will later regret."[1] In different words, Dad echoed the wisdom of James: "My dear brothers and sisters, take note of this: Everyone should be quick to listen, slow to speak and slow to become angry, because human anger does not produce the righteousness that God desires" (James 1:19–20). What Dad said seemed like good advice so I put my phone down—*I didn't make the call.*

One day went by and I didn't make the call. I was still too angry.

Two days went by and I didn't make the call. I was still too angry.

It was not until a week later that I was in a peaceful, calm, healthy, and even loving place to call this person. After all, this person too is loved by God.

I have joked that this is how I know that Dad was so much more spiritually mature than I was: *he only needed 24 hours while I*

---

1. At some point in my 30s, Dad started calling me "B."

needed a week! Jokes aside, his advice was golden and another talk that profoundly impacted my life. Aware of my Dad's advice along with my tendencies, my wife challenges me from time to time to wait at least 24 hours before I respond to someone when I am either hurt or angry. Whether through speech, chat, or email, allowing some time to pass gives the Holy Spirit the space to work in my heart so that I do not sin against the Lord. Dad died years ago, but his words are still guiding me in both my personal and professional life.

8

You Can't Break What is Broken

THE OTHER DAY, THE "S" key on my Apple keyboard was not working. Given that I work online, I need that key. After a few days of frustration, I decided to buy a new Apple keyboard which would cost around $100.

Before I got around to ordering it, it dawned on me that I had not even tried to fix it. I had never removed a key from an Apple keyboard and was not sure if it would snap back on. But what did I have to lose? If it worked, I would save $100. If not, I would be no worse off. So, I decided to give it a shot. I took my pocket knife, slid it under the key, and popped it off the keyboard. Once it was removed, I immediately discovered a hairball that had been keeping the plastic key from engaging when I pressed it. I cleaned out the space, successfully snapped the key back onto the keyboard, and am pleased to announce that it worked perfectly.

While I am sure that you did not buy this book to hear my Apple keyboard story, this experience reminded me of something Dad shared years ago. I was in my early 30s at the time, and my wife and I were living in the first home we bought, the same home where the previous story in this book took place (Wait 24 Hours). At one point, our dryer suddenly stopped working. It would turn on and sound normal, but it did not dry our clothes—there was no heat. It was early in our marriage and there was very little money left at the end of the month after paying bills. So, the possibility of buying a new dryer was very discouraging. For this reason, I decided to call Dad rather than hastily purchase a new dryer on credit.

Dad was a jack-of-all-trades, so I always called him when something was broken. He possessed an uncanny ability to fix things. He is the same guy that my grandfather hired to be his diesel mechanic at Taylor Propane, even though Dad had no experience. He had an 18-wheeler brought to the shop and told Dad to take the entire engine apart and then put it back together and that once he completed this task, he would know how engines work. This is exactly what Dad did, and when he was done, he knew the parts of the engine and how they worked. He became a phenomenal mechanic. Needless to say, he was the type of man who either knew how to do something or could easily learn.

Dad answered my phone call and I told him about the dryer. I can't remember the entire conversation, but at one point he said: "B.J., you already have a dryer that doesn't work, so why not take it apart and at least see if you notice anything wrong? *You can't break what is broken.*" He explained that the problem was likely with the heating element, and if that was the case, it would be a relatively easy fix.

After the phone call, I removed the back paneling on the dryer and located the heating element. As it turned out, there was a clean break in the coil. I purchased the part and was able to easily install it myself.

This practical philosophy—*you can't break what is broken*—has since helped me on numerous occasions. A couple of years ago, our oven stopped working. We were unable to use the "Bake" or "Broil" option, and this was even more of an issue since we pride ourselves on not having a microwave. This had to be fixed! My good friend, the internet, suggested that the circuit board (not sure of the exact name of the part) might be the problem. I purchased one online and installed it once it arrived. It worked!

You Can't Break What is Broken

The fact of the matter is that I am not the handyman that my Dad was. I doubt anyone will dispute this claim. For this reason, I have always been much more reluctant to take things apart and see if I can fix them. This is why Dad's practical advice—*you can't break what is broken*—has proved so helpful to me. If you unsuccessfully try to fix something that is already broken, you only end up where you started: *with something that does not work*.

9

Setting Me Free

Years ago, I was struck by something that Henry David Thoreau wrote in *Walden*. *Walden* is a reflective account of the author's two-year experiment living in solitude near Walden Pond in Massachusetts. During these two years, he lived simply in nature to gain deeper insights into life and society. Toward the beginning of the book, Thoreau writes:

> I see young men, my townsmen, whose misfortune it is to have inherited farms, houses, barns, cattle, and farming tools; for these are more easily acquired than got rid of. Better if they had been born in the open pasture and suckled by a wolf, that they might have seen with clearer eyes what field they were called to labor in.[1]

While an inheritance can be a blessing, Thoreau's point is powerful—*an inheritance can also enslave*. It can bind one to feel obligated to spend life—*one's only life*—ignoring what is in one's deep heart in order to do what is given and expected. Thankfully, my Dad used his words in the story I will now tell to ensure that I did not fall prey to such a tragedy.

---

1. Thoreau, *Walden*, 2.

Unlike the stories I have told thus far, I cannot remember the exact details of this talk. Yet, I do remember the talk and it might have occurred more than once. It was about Grace Fellowship and who would pastor the church after him. Without this talk, I am not sure how I would have felt about the senior pastor vacancy that immediately opened when he died since I am the oldest son and someone who has spent years in vocational ministry.

After I graduated with my B.A. in Psychology and another in Philosophy at the University of Missouri - Kansas City, I returned to Texas to serve under my Dad's leadership. The name of the church is Grace Fellowship Ministries and my family, along with a few others, started the church. I was 25 at the time and served there until I was 27. On one occasion, Dad was out of town and a group of men were preparing to build the stage. They were trying to decide on the appropriate height. I called Dad and he simply replied, "You can make the decision. Do what you think looks best." I got off the phone and told the man standing there that Dad had told me that I can make the decision. I will never forget his response: "Well, it will be your stage anyway one day. It might as well be you that chooses the height." I vividly remember this catching me off-guard. Is this the Lord's will? Will I spend my entire life in Winnsboro, Texas? Honestly, I thought he was wrong. I am not the person. I also remember thinking: "This guy has the wrong son. It is my brother that will pastor this church one day." At the time of this writing, neither my brother nor I pastor the church, and God is blessing the work under the current leadership.

During my time at Grace Fellowship, I am guessing that most people probably thought that I was my Dad's heir. It made sense. I could serve for years and eventually take over when I had matured and learned from him. But in my heart, I never really thought that I was the person to follow Dad. Yet, as an oldest son, it would have been somewhat difficult for me if Dad had believed otherwise.

I remember asking Dad at some point—probably during those years of serving as a youth pastor at Grace Fellowship—if he expected me to take over for him one day. I wanted an honest answer. I remember telling him that although I saw the church's role in the Kingdom as important and worthy of a lifetime commitment, I did not feel it was my calling. I did not sense that it was part of God's long-term plan for my life.

While the conversation was brief, Dad made it clear that he did not expect me to follow in his shoes. He went a step further and affirmed that he did not think it was part of what God had for me. While pastoring and preaching brought my Dad great joy, the former had also caused him great pain. His heart had been bruised and tattered over time. He did not want the same for me. Dad set me free in that conversation. I never had to live with the feeling that Dad expected and desired something of me that was not in my heart. By making this known in conversation, he set me free to follow what God planted in my heart. His actions also make another truth clear: *Dad ultimately viewed me as God's property, not his own.* He was there to steward, not control or manipulate. Therefore, when Dad tragically died and went to be with the Lord, I was able to officiate his funeral, honor his memory, grieve with loved ones, and then return to Scotland to finish my Ph.D. studies rather than do something out of guilt or a false sense of obligation. Writing this makes me long for one more moment with Dad to thank him for all that he did to ensure that I could follow the Lord peacefully and joyfully.

10

The Book We Started

A FEW YEARS AGO, Dad and I decided to write a book together. We created a Google Document and I began to ask questions to prompt his thinking and provide some organization to the project. I cannot remember for sure, but we may have decided to write it more as an interview where I would ask certain questions and he would respond. Whatever the form, I would play a secondary role, serving Dad in whatever way that I could to help him write.

The book he longed to write was for pastors of small churches. He knew their challenges, heartaches, and joy. He knew all too well that while a church split might not be felt as deeply in a larger church, it was devastating in a small congregation. Simply put, Dad knew the ups and downs of pastoring a small congregation, and he wanted to draw from his experience and write a book that would speak to the *hidden* pastors.

Honestly, I do not know if we would have ever finished the book. I remember suggesting changes at one point because his writing mirrored his speaking style too closely. As many writers know, speaking and writing are distinct art forms with different techniques. After I made the corrections, he mentioned in our next conversation that I had essentially eliminated his voice. He said something like: "B.J., this is the way that I write."

I wanted to say: "Yes, I'm aware. I am here to help."

It might have been a hopeless endeavor, but the document remained. By the end of the book, one of us would have loved it and the other would have probably wanted their name removed! All jokes aside, the message in Dad's heart was beautiful and carried the weight and authority of that which is born in pain.

In Dad's defense, this was a rough draft. He never had the chance to go back and clean things up. That said, I do not want to change anything now that he has passed. So, here are the exact words that Dad wrote in the document we were using for a rough draft:

> Let me begin by saying that not only is writing a book with a son that I am so very proud of a wonderful privilege, but it is also an opportunity to encourage other pastors. I have been in the senior pastor role for almost 29 years. I have pastored denominational churches and now pastor a non-denominational church that I began 24 years ago. I'm not sure of all the subjects we will deal with but I will begin with saying I believe anyone pastoring a church under 150 in attendance each week is my hero.
>
> I have not always been a pastor. I surrendered to the ministry at about the age of 30 and soon after became a senior pastor (that poor church). I thought I was going to change the world from the podium of my first church. I remember one Wednesday evening I had 1 in attendance besides my family. Talk about small beginnings! But I had a dream.
>
> My prayer is that God will use this book to bring life back to some of those forgotten dreams and desires that we as pastors have in our hearts. Maybe in some way this will help you to know that you do not have to pastor a megachurch to "count." Hopefully you will understand that by you holding the hand of that Mom and Dad that have just lost a child is just as important in God's scheme of things as preaching 6 services on Sunday morning to several thousand.
>
> Simply put, my heart is to help rescue pastors and their wives who are about to throw in the towel and call it

quits. Let me say to you: God, this world, and that church you are in need you....because you count!

I then gave Dad the following prompt:

Dad, let's take a minute to tell pastors (and anyone reading this book) a little bit about who you are. Where do you live? How small is the town? What is the name of the church that you pastor? On average, how many people attend your services every Sunday? After you provide some biographical information, we can move on to the good stuff.

Within a few days, he responded:

Ok, let me see if I can put who I am in words that make sense. I was called to preach when I was 16 but said no, thought I had a better plan; I was going to be rich and I knew enough at the time to figure out preaching wouldn't get me there. But then at about 29 through complications with the birth of my daughter, I surrendered my all to what God wanted. He once again issued the call to preach, and this time I said YES! I pastored in a denominational setting for 7 years and then 24 years ago we started Grace Fellowship Ministries.
The town I pastor in has a population of about 3500. The thing about pastoring in a small town is that everyone knows everyone else's business...no really. Small church and small town pastoring is in my opinion, one of the most difficult jobs on earth. Right now we average about 140 in Sunday morning attendance. I hope later in the book to share some of the ups and downs of the last 30 years, a heartbreaking church split, and many more of the challenges that are present in a "small church" setting.

Next he jotted down a few of the chapter headings:

1. Pastor, Plumber, Yard Man, Secretary: Keeping the Right Perspective
2. I Quit Mondays
3. Big Ideas, Small Budget

4. Admitting Failure: Learning How to Shift to Reverse
5. Preaching to 30 like It's 3000: Staying Passionate

When I read this list, I am struck by the down-to-earth, humble, and relevant nature of the chapters. I wish Dad would have lived long enough to write this book. Just one glance at the list of chapters reveals his heart and that he had first-hand knowledge of the ups and downs of small church ministry. There is no doubt in my mind that his words would have been fresh wind and cool waters to hurting pastors.

While this chapter is different from the other chapters that focus on Billy Condrey as a father, it nonetheless is another window into his heart. It is always helpful to see things from multiple perspectives. Whether a husband, parent, pastor, or aspiring writer, Dad loved well and sought to help others with his words. Along with so many other things, I will never understand why God took him so suddenly with so much left in his heart. C.S. Lewis, one of my favorites authors, writes:

> When I lay these questions before God I get no answer. But rather a special sort of "No answer." It is not the locked door. It is more like a silent, certainly not uncompassionate, gaze. As though He shook His head not in refusal but waving the question. Like, "Peace, child; you don't understand."[1]

Dad's departure is a reminder of what this book is about. None of us will live on this earth forever. We will die. In his letter to the Ephesians, Paul writes: "Do not let any unwholesome talk come out of your mouths, but only what is helpful for building others up according to their needs, that it may benefit those who listen" (Eph. 4:29). For those of us who have used our words in a loving, wise, and timely manner—especially with our children—something of us will remain that will continue to take root, blossom, and create life and beauty in those we love. This is what my Dad did, and it made all the difference.

---

1. Lewis, *A Grief Observed*, 685.

11

A Final Word

WHEN YOU FIRST SET out to write a book, you never know what will transpire during the writing process. Four days ago, I returned from the funeral of my Dad's mother in Texas. Her name was Mary Ruth—*we called her RuRu*. She was five days away from turning 90 when she passed. She was kind, strong, steadfast, persevering, and loving. In many ways, she embodied the character of Ruth in the Bible. She loved Jesus, met continually with other women for Bible study, had a strong group of friends, and knew both joy and suffering.

When I received the phone call that she had died, I spent the next hour crying off and on. I knew that I would be sad when she passed, but I was not expecting the level of grief I experienced. After a few minutes, I knew what was happening: *I was grieving the loss of my Dad once again.* In some strange sense, RuRu's death made me feel like yet another piece of Dad had died. His death was somehow more final, more solidified—*even the pieces of him that remained were now disappearing.* RuRu's passing meant that more of Dad was gone. I am not sure how this sounds, but I have learned with grief that it does not help to overthink or overanalyze. It is best to simply allow yourself to feel and then work through those feelings.

In my mind, RuRu's death is another good reason to write this book about Dad. If more of him is missing from the earth, then what better time to tell a few choice stories than now? While time passes, this book is a reminder that the time we take with our children, the moments we stop to look them in the eye, and the words that we speak will outlive us. These humble speech acts in the mundane hours of life are quite possibly the most precious of all. You never know when a normal metal will be turned to gold. *Maybe parents are the only true alchemists!*

Bibliography

Dobson, James. *Bringing Up Boys*. Wheaton, IL: Tyndale House, 2001.
Frankl, Viktor. *Man's Search for Meaning*. 3rd ed. Translated by Ilse Lasch. New York, NY: Simon & Schuster, 1984.
Grenz, Stanley, and Jay T. Smith. "Integrity." In *Pocket Dictionary of Ethics*. The IVP Pocket Reference Series. Downers Grove, IL: InterVarsity Press, 2003.
Kakinami, Lisa, Tracie A. Barnett, Louise Séguin, and Gilles Paradis. "Parenting Style and Obesity Risk in Children." Preventive Medicine 75 (2015): 18–22.
Lambert, Tom. *Dad's Playbook*. San Francisco, CA: Chronicle Books, 2012.
Lewis, C.S. *The Four Loves*. In *The C.S. Lewis Signature Classics*, 739–836. New York, NY: HarperOne, 2017.
———. *A Grief Observed*. In *The C.S. Lewis Signature Classics*, 647–688. New York, NY: HarperOne, 2017.
Mason, Charlotte. *A Philosophy of Education*. Home Education Series. Living Book Press, 2017.
Myers, David and C. Nathan DeWall. *Psychology in Everyday Life*. 5th ed. New York, NY: Bedford, Freeman & Worth, 2020.
Nelson, Candance. "The 4 Types of Parenting Styles: What Style is Right for You?" May 10, 2023, https://mcpress.mayoclinic.org/parenting/what-parenting-style-is-right-for-you/#:~:text=There%20are%20four%20main%20parenting,leaves%20no%20room%20for%20negotiation..
Nouwen, Henri J.M. *The Living Reminder*. New York, NY: Seabury Press, 1977.
Nuwer, Rachel. "When Becoming a Man Means Sticking Your Hand Into a Glove of Ants." October 27, 2014, https://www.smithsonianmag.com/smart-news/brazilian-tribe-becoming-man-requires-sticking-your-hand-glove-full-angry-ants-180953156/.
Sanvictores, Terrence, and Magda D. Mendez. "Types of Parenting Styles and Effects On Children." Last modified September 18, 2022. National Library of Medicine. Accessed June 1, 2014. https://www.ncbi.nlm.nih.gov/books/NBK568743/.
Thompson, Francis. "The Hound of Heaven." Accessed June 1, 2024. http://www.houndofheaven.com/poem.

BIBLIOGRAPHY

Thoreau, Henry D. *Walden*. New York: Fall River Press, 2017.

Willard, Dallas. *The Divine Conspiracy*. New York, NY: HarperCollins Publishers, 2009. Kindle.

www.ingramcontent.com/pod-product-compliance
Lightning Source LLC
Chambersburg PA
CBHW060430050426
42449CB00009B/2217